£7.99

One Direction

A 2015 Annual

Written by Becky Bowden

Designed by Duncan Cook

Contents

One Direction

Intro

Meet One Direction. A boy band whose name is instantly recognisable all around the world, thanks to their ever-expanding list of hit singles, chart-topping albums and boyish good looks. One Direction are of course made up of the very lovely: Niall Horan, Zayn Malik, Liam Payne, Harry Styles and Louis Tomlinson.

Together these chart-topping superstars have successfully managed to prove that with a lot of hard work, a fiercely loyal fan base and some seriously catchy tunes, it is still possible to maintain a long and prosperous career in the music industry today, no matter what your musical style might be. The lads have

released everything from soppy ballads to upbeat and catchy tracks and have successfully topped the charts with them all. These past couple of years have been some of their busiest yet and they certainly show no signs of slowing down any time soon. They are always heavily involved in charity work in one way or another and always make time to give back to those less fortunate than themselves, making them seem even more down to earth, despite their obvious mega-fame.

Between them, they have racked up millions of followers on all of the top social media sites, with their fans and supporters travelling from all over the world to catch a glimpse of their favourite band performing live on stage. One Direction have released fragrances, calendars, books and even a movie and we have a sneaky suspicion that this is just the very tip of the iceberg for this talented and driven young band. Niall, Zayn, Liam, Harry and Louis

have surpassed everyone's expectations following the early days of their careers on *The X Factor* and have gone on to build a credible name for themselves with both fans and the music industry itself. Having been signed to Simon Cowell's 'Syco' record label, the boys are lucky enough to have worked with Simon himself as well as some of the hottest musical talent the world has ever seen. From famous producers to cutting edge musicians and celebrity 'royalty' One Direction have spent time with everyone who is anyone throughout the course of their exciting, high-flying career.

Keep reading to find out everything you need to know about One Direction, along with plenty of interactive puzzles, a fun 'mega quiz' and glossy pictures galore of your favourite boys.

Then and Now

When One Direction first hit the music scene in 2010 it was as part of the hugely successful seventh series of popular TV show *The X Factor* in the UK.

No-one could have predicted the success that this group of five young lads would have or the changes that would take place in their lives as a result of this long-running series.

Have you noticed just how much One Direction have changed as their career progressed? Take a look at some of the top changes from then to now.

Looks

It goes without saying that the boys have all changed significantly since their first appearance on *The X Factor*. They are all older, more mature and really seem

to have found their own sense of style both as a band and in their individual looks. One Direction are a band who don't always look perfectly preened and polished and instead have developed

their own unique sense of style. They just instinctively know what looks good on them for various different events and occasions.

They've completely nailed it with their ability to go from sporting a casual everyday outfit to a slick, sophisticated suit in the blink of an eye and make both look equally good, don't you think?

Personalities

All of the One Direction boys seem to have blossomed throughout the process of shaping their successful careers. Harry has perhaps always had an air of natural confidence surrounding him, but the rest of the boys appear to have caught up

pretty quickly and have come a long way from the often shy and reserved stage presence that can be seen in a couple of their very early performances.

All members of One Direction seem to have now mellowed in to their new found fame and come across as accepting and grateful for the opportunities that

have aged, their voices have also matured and their song choices are varied and well thought out. Their newer tracks such as 'You and I' definitely show a more mature side to the band as they evolve and experiment with new styles.

Status

This must be one of the biggest changes for Liam, Harry, Louis, Niall and Zayn, both individually and as a group. They went from being just your average guys next door, to being internationally adored in just a few short months.

One Direction now have the world at their fingertips and have a host of celebrity friends, fancy houses and fast cars. These guys have worked hard for the changes that they have been lucky enough to experience though and it never looks as though they are taking it all for granted. Keep doing what you're doing, guys!

they are presented with. They have certainly blossomed into a group of cool, confident guys who know how to make the most of this exciting time in their lives and have transported the fans along on this epic journey.

Music

Musically the band seem to be much more in control of what they put out there these days and they have definitely found what suits their individual voices best. As they

Profile

Harry Styles

Harry Styles was born on February 1, 1994 in Worcestershire. He has been hugely into music from a young age  and is no stranger to performing on stage. Harry attended Holmes Chapel Comprehensive School. During his time there he and a group of close friends formed their first band - White Eskimo - with Harry as the lead singer. The band were so popular with fellow students that they even won a competition!

Harry once worked part time at a bakery in his spare time during weekends and after school, but has come a long way since then, thanks to a very wise last minute decision to audition for *The X Factor* that saw him shoot to fame along with his fellow One Direction band-mates.

Name: Harry Edward Styles

Date of Birth: 1 February 1994. He is the youngest member of One Direction.

Place of Birth: Worcestershire. Harry later moved to Holmes Chapel, Cheshire.

Star Sign: Aquarius

Instruments He Can Play: The kazoo

Siblings: One sister called Gemma

Favourite Colour: Blue or orange

Official Twitter Account: @Harry_Styles

Profile

Liam Payne

Liam Payne is one of the biggest success stories of *The X Factor* to date, proving that you should never, ever give up on your dreams! He  first auditioned for *The X Factor* back in 2008 but didn't quite make it as far as he had hoped in the competition. However, this may have all been a blessing in disguise, as two years later in 2010, Liam returned for another crack at fame, during the show's seventh series. This time, the judges combined him with four other guys (Louis, Harry, Niall and Zayn) to form a 'super group' that would eventually be known as One Direction.

Name: Liam James Payne

Date of Birth: 29 August 1993

Place of Birth: Wolverhampton, West Midlands

Star Sign: Virgo

Instruments He Can Play: Piano and guitar

Siblings: Two older sisters

Favourite Colour: Purple or blue

Official Twitter Account: @Real_Liam_Payne

Profile

Louis Tomlinson

Louis Tomlinson was perhaps always destined for big things in the world of entertainment. He was no stranger to stage and screen after minor roles on hit UK TV shows *Waterloo Road*, *Fat Friends* and *If I Had You*.

Born in Doncaster, South Yorkshire to parents Johannah and Troy Austin, Louis took his stepfather Mark Tomlinson's name after his parents divorced. The judges placed Louis into a group with Liam, Harry, Zayn and Niall after he auditioned for *The X Factor* in 2010 and he hasn't looked back since!

Name: Louis William Tomlinson, born Louis Troy Austin

Date of Birth: 24 December 1991. Louis is the oldest member of the group.

Place of Birth: Doncaster, South Yorkshire

Star Sign: Capricorn

Instruments he can play: Piano

Siblings: One half-brother and six younger half-sisters

Favourite Colour: Red

Official Twitter Account: @Louis_Tomlinson

Profile

Zayn Malik

Zayn Malik was born on January 12, 1993 and is of English and Pakistani descent. He showed an early love of entertaining, taking performing arts courses and appearing in school productions.

Zayn has often described himself as being a bit of a hyperactive child growing up – he always had plenty of energy! That must certainly be working to his advantage now. After auditioning for *The X Factor* back in 2010 he joined one of the biggest boy-bands ever. Now he has a job that involves jumping around on stage and travelling all over the world!

Full Name: Zain Javadd 'Zayn' Malik

Date of Birth: 12 January 1993

Place of Birth: Bradford, West Yorkshire

Star Sign: Capricorn

Siblings: Zayn has three sisters – an older sister called Doniya, and two younger sisters called Waliyha and Safaa.

Favourite Colour: Red and blue

Official Twitter Account: @zaynmalik

Profile

Niall Horan

Niall has been interested in music for as long as he can remember. From the age of eleven he'd sit in his bedroom and  write songs and he has spent years learning how to play the guitar. He auditioned for *The X Factor* in 2010 and became one of the members of a new group, put together by the judges themselves. Along with fellow band-mates Harry, Louis, Liam and Zayn, One Direction was eventually born. Since then, Niall has described himself as 'literally the luckiest person in the world' for the successful career they all now enjoy.

Full Name: Niall James Horan

Date of Birth: 13 September 1993

Place of Birth: Mullingar, County Westmeath, Ireland

Star Sign: Virgo

Instruments he can play: Guitar

Siblings: An older brother called Greg

Favourite Colour: Green or blue

Official Twitter Account: @NiallOfficial

Anagrams

How quickly can you unmuddle these One Direction song titles?

1. Events or begs

4. Scald better skill

2. Tighten still

7. Mum resolve

5. Yet go about

3. If fool mystery

8. I retire bliss

6. On the warlord

9. Star silk fists

ANSWERS ON PAGE 60

Highlights *from* the Past Year

2014 has been a busy year for One Direction. They've had loads of fantastic moments, but here are five of the best!

Hit Singles

In 2014 One Direction released the hit singles *Midnight Memories* and *You and I*. Both were hugely popular with fans worldwide. The video for *You and I* was especially popular due to its creative 'freeze frame' style effect!

Where We Are Tour

The *Where We Are* tour was one of One Direction's biggest and best yet, proving to be a great highlight for the band. The concert tour officially kicked off on 25 April 2014 at El Campin Stadium in Bogota, Colombia and promotes the band's third studio album, *Midnight Memories*.

Radio 1's Big Weekend

The band played a fantastic set at Radio 1's Big Weekend in Glasgow and left fans going wild for more! Also performing at the event were their showbiz pals Ed Sheeran and Pharrell Williams, making for an electric atmosphere all round.

What have been your personal One Direction highlights from the past year? We've left space below for you to write your own!

Stealing the Show at the Brit Awards

One Direction took the 2014 Brit Awards by storm and walked away with the awards for Global Success and Best British Video for *Best Song Ever*. A real career highlight for the lads that further showcased their ever-growing popularity.

Taking Over Kids' TV

Harry and Liam made their *Sesame Street* TV debut to sing *The Alphabet Song* with Bert. The show has seen many of Hollywood's A-list stars appear and One Direction were quick to accept their invitation to be part of the fun!

Wordsearch

All of the below words are related to One Direction somehow. Can you find them hidden within the grid? You can find and check the answers at the back of the book.

Words can go horizontally, vertically and diagonally in all eight directions.

```
K O G B D L F T Z L E B G K L Z M C
Y U N M N Y O U A N D I T R F W L N
N R L J Y T X D Y Z Y B N R D J S N
O M O N C K C A R K M W L W G E X S
I O N T N R P T G A H Q P W I M R U
T M D T C O C Y S E W O Y R M Q F S
C E O B T A Z R R H N A O V M K L I
E N N Z N Q F E Z E O M T M H C Q S
R T T G L W W X T V E R N I A D M I
I S M V L E T H E M D O A M R L M H
D E Z Y A N I J T H S R T N H B I T
E L K R R N R H M N T R H F P J T K
N Y E J G Z G N I T M C Z Q X Y N T
O T X F Q I B L Q K L F N W Z C M J
F S Y J N K M J L K I S S Y O U T N
M Y G D L O L I T T L E T H I N G S
T D I K T Q H G X J W K C F J K B M
K M Z J C G D N E K E E W G I B H H
```

BIGWEEKEND	OURMOMENT
BRITAWARD	PAYNE
HORAN	STYLES
KISSYOU	SYCO
LITTLETHINGS	THEXFACTOR
LONDON	THISISUS
MALIK	TOMLINSON
MIDNIGHTMEMORIES	WHEREWEARE
ONEDIRECTION	YOUANDI
ONETHING	

ANSWERS ON PAGE 60

Spot the Difference

Take a look at the two images below - can you spot the six differences between them?

ANSWERS ON PAGE 60

The Tours! O₂ arena

London O₂ Aren

If there's one thing that One Direction know how to do, it's put on a show-stopping tour! Harry, Niall, Louis, Liam and Zayn have travelled around the world, bringing their most-loved hit songs to their army of adoring fans and putting on a show to remember in the process. If you've ever been to a One Direction concert, you'll know exactly what we mean.

The 'Up All Night' Tour (2011–12)

The 'Up All Night' tour ran during 2011-2012 and was One Direction's first headlining world tour. The boys pulled out all the stops to ensure that it was a huge success and to show everyone what they were really made of!

Where they played:

18	December	2011	Watford, **England** – Watford Colosseum
19	December	2011	Westcliff-on-Sea – Cliffs Pavilion
21	December	2011	Wolverhampton – Wolverhampton Civic Hall
22	December	2011	Manchester – O2 Apollo Manchester
23	December	2011	Manchester – O2 Apollo Manchester
3	January	2012	Bournemouth – Bournemouth International Centre
4	January	2012	Birmingham – National Indoor Arena
5	January	2012	Plymouth – Plymouth Pavilions
7	January	2012	Nottingham – Nottingham Royal Concert Hall
8	January	2012	Brighton – Brighton Centre
10	January	2012	London – HMV Hammersmith Apollo
11	January	2012	London – HMV Hammersmith Apollo
13	January	2012	Glasgow, **Scotland** – Clyde Auditorium
14	January	2012	Glasgow – Clyde Auditorium
15	January	2012	Liverpool, **England** – Echo Arena Liverpool
17	January	2012	Newcastle – Newcastle City Hall
18	January	2012	Blackpool – Blackpool Opera House
20	January	2012	Sheffield – Sheffield City Hall
21	January	2012	Cardiff, **Wales** – Motorpoint Arena Cardiff
22	January	2012	London, **England** – HMV Hammersmith Apollo
24	January	2012	Dublin, **Ireland** – The O2
25	January	2012	Belfast, **Northern Ireland** – Waterfront Hall
26	January	2012	Belfast – Waterfront Hall
13	April	2012	Sydney, **Australia** – Hordern Pavilion
16	April	2012	Melbourne – Hisense Arena
18	April	2012	Brisbane – BBEC Great Hall
21	April	2012	Auckland, **New Zealand** – Trusts Stadium
22	April	2012	Wellington – St. James Theatre
22	May	2012	Uncasville, **USA** – Mohegan Sun Arena
24	May	2012	Fairfax – Patriot Centre
25	May	2012	East Rutherford – Izod Center
26	May	2012	New York City – Beacon Theatre
28	May	2012	Camden – Susquehanna Bank Center
29	May	2012	Toronto, **Canada** – Molson Canadian Amphitheatre
31	May	2012	Toronto – Molson Canadian Amphitheatre
1	June	2012	Detroit, **USA** – Fox Theatre
2	June	2012	Rosemont – Allstate Arena
5	June	2012	Mexico City, **Mexico** – Auditorio Nacional
6	June	2012	Mexico City – Auditorio Nacional
8	June	2012	San Diego, **USA** – Viejas Arena
9	June	2012	Las Vegas – Theatre for the Performing Arts
10	June	2012	Phoenix – Comerica Theatre
13	June	2012	San Jose – Event Center Arena
14	June	2012	Oakland – Paramount Theatre
16	June	2012	Los Angeles – Gibson Amphitheatre
17	June	2012	Anaheim – The Theatre at Honda Center
23	June	2012	Dallas – Gexa Energy Pavilion
24	June	2012	The Woodlands – Cynthia Woods Mitchell Pavilion
26	June	2012	Duluth Arena at Gwinnett Center
27	June	2012	Charlotte – Time Warner Cable Arena
29	June	2012	Tampa – 1-800-Ask-Gary Amphitheatre
30	June	2012	Orlando – Amway Center
1	July	2012	Fort Lauderdale – Bank Atlantic Center

Sydney

The 'Take Me Home' Tour (2013)

Toronto - Rogers Centre

The 'Take Me Home' tour was One Direction's second worldwide headlining tour, in 2013. They played some amazing countries and venues and continued to put on an even bigger and better show for fans as their popularity spiralled.

Where they played:

23	February	2013	London, **England** – The O2 Arena
24	February	2013	London – The O2 Arena
26	February	2013	Glasgow **Scotland** – Scottish Exhibition and Conference Centre
27	February	2013	Glasgow – Scottish Exhibition and Conference Centre
1	March	2013	Cardiff, **Wales** – Motorpoint Arena Cardiff
2	March	2013	Cardiff – Motorpoint Arena Cardiff
5	March	2013	Dublin, **Ireland** – The O2
6	March	2013	Dublin – The O2
7	March	2013	Belfast, Northern Ireland – Odyssey Arena
8	March	2013	Belfast – Odyssey Arena
10	March	2013	Belfast – Odyssey Arena
11	March	2013	Belfast – Odyssey Arena
12	March	2013	Dublin, **Ireland** – The O2
13	March	2013	Dublin – The O2
15	March	2013	Manchester, **England** – Manchester Arena
16	March	2013	Manchester – Manchester Arena
17	March	2013	Liverpool – Echo Arena Liverpool
19	March	2013	Sheffield – Motorpoint Arena Sheffield
20	March	2013	Nottingham – Capital FM Arena
22	March	2013	Birmingham – LG Arena
23	March	2013	Birmingham – LG Arena
31	March	2013	Liverpool – Echo Arena Liverpool
1	April	2013	London – The O2 Arena
2	April	2013	London – The O2 Arena
4	April	2013	London – The O2 Arena
5	April	2013	London – The O2 Arena
6	April	2013	London – The O2 Arena
8	April	2013	Newcastle – Metro Radio Arena
9	April	2013	Newcastle – Metro Radio Arena
10	April	2013	Newcastle – Metro Radio Arena
12	April	2013	Glasgow, **Scotland** – Scottish Exhibition and Conference Centre
13	April	2013	Sheffield, **England** – Motorpoint Arena
14	April	2013	Sheffield – Motorpoint Arena
16	April	2013	Nottingham – Capital FM Arena
17	April	2013	Birmingham – LG Arena
19	April	2013	Manchester – Manchester Arena
20	April	2013	Manchester – Manchester Arena
29	April	2013	Paris, **France** – Palais Omnisports de Paris-Bercy
30	April	2013	Metz – Galaxie Amneville
1	May	2013	Antwerp, **Belgium** – Sportpaleis
3	May	2013	Amsterdam, **Netherlands** – Ziggo Dome
4	May	2013	Oberhausen, **Germany** – Konig Pilsener Arena
5	May	2013	Herning, **Denmark** – Jyske Bank Boxen
7	May	2013	Bærum, **Norway** – Telenor Arena
8	May	2013	Stockholm, **Sweden** – Friends Arena
10	May	2013	Copenhagen, **Denmark** – Forum Arena
11	May	2013	Berlin, **Germany** – O2 World Berlin
12	May	2013	Hamburg – O2 World Hamburg
16	May	2013	Zurich, **Switzerland** – Hallenstadion
17	May	2013	Munich, **Germany** – Olympiahalle
19	May	2013	Verona, **Italy** – Verona Arena
20	May	2013	Milan – Mediolanum Forum
22	May	2013	Barcelona, **Spain** – Palau Municipal d'Esports
24	May	2013	Madrid – Palacio Vistalegre
25	May	2013	Madrid – Palacio Vistalegre
26	May	2013	Lisbon, **Portugal** – MEO Arena
8	June	2013	Mexico City, **Mexico** – Foro Sol
9	June	2013	Mexico City – Foro Sol
13	June	2013	Sunrise, **USA** – BB&T Center
14	June	2013	Miami – American Airlines Arena
16	June	2013	Louisville – KFC Yum! Center
18	June	2013	Columbus – Nationwide Arena
19	June	2013	Nashville – Bridgestone Arena
21	June	2013	Atlanta – Philips Arena
22	June	2013	Raleigh – PNC Arena
23	June	2013	Washington D.C. – Verizon Center
25	June	2013	Philadelphia – Wells Fargo Center
26	June	2013	Mansfield – Comcast Center
28	June	2013	Wantagh – Nikon at Jones Beach Theater
29	June	2013	Wantagh – Nikon at Jones Beach Theater
2	July	2013	East Rutherford – Izod Center
4	July	2013	Montreal, **Canada** – Bell Centre
5	July	2013	Hershey, **USA** – Hersheypark Stadium
6	July	2013	Hershey – Hersheypark Stadium
8	July	2013	Pittsburgh – Consol Energy Center
9	July	2013	Toronto, **Canada** – Air Canada Centre
10	July	2013	Toronto – Air Canada Centre
12	July	2013	Auburn Hills, **USA** – The Palace of Auburn Hills
13	July	2013	Tinley Park – First Midwest Bank Amphitheatre
14	July	2013	Tinley Park – First Midwest Bank Amphitheatre
18	July	2013	Minneapolis – Target Center
19	July	2013	Kansas City – Sprint Center
21	July	2013	Houston – Toyota Center
22	July	2013	Dallas – American Airlines Center
24	July	2013	Denver – Pepsi Center
25	July	2013	West Valley City – Maverik Center
27	July	2013	Vancouver, **Canada** – Rogers Arena
28	July	2013	Seattle, **USA** – KeyArena
30	July	2013	San Jose – SAP Center
31	July	2013	Oakland – Oracle Arena
2	August	2013	Las Vegas Mandalay Bay Events Center
3	August	2013	Las Vegas Mandalay Bay Events Center
4	August	2013	Chula Vista – Sleep Train Amphitheatre
7	August	2013	Los Angeles – Staples Center

Stockholm

Lima - Estadio Naciona

8	August	2013	Los Angeles – Staples Center
9	August	2013	Los Angeles – Staples Center
10	August	2013	Los Angeles – Staples Center
23	September	2013	Adelaide, **Australia** – Adelaide Entertainment Centre
24	September	2013	Adelaide – Adelaide Entertainment Centre
25	September	2013	Adelaide – Adelaide Entertainment Centre
28	September	2013	Perth – Perth Arena
29	September	2013	Perth – Perth Arena
2	October	2013	Melbourne – Rod Laver Arena
3	October	2013	Melbourne – Rod Laver Arena
5	October	2013	Sydney – Allphones Arena
6	October	2013	Sydney – Allphones Arena
10	October	2013	Christchurch, **New Zealand** – CBS Canterbury Arena
12	October	2013	Auckland – Vector Arena
13	October	2013	Auckland – Vector Arena
16	October	2013	Melbourne, **Australia** – Rod Laver Arena
17	October	2013	Melbourne – Rod Laver Arena
19	October	2013	Brisbane – Brisbane Entertainment Centre
20	October	2013	Brisbane – Brisbane Entertainment Centre
21	October	2013	Brisbane – Brisbane Entertainment Centre
23	October	2013	Sydney – Allphones Arena
24	October	2013	Sydney – Allphones Arena
25	October	2013	Sydney – Allphones Arena
26	October	2013	Sydney – Allphones Arena
28	October	2013	Melbourne – Rod Laver Arena
29	October	2013	Melbourne – Rod Laver Arena
30	October	2013	Melbourne – Rod Laver Arena
2	November	2013	Tokyo, **Japan** – Makuhari Messe

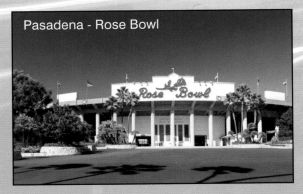
Pasadena - Rose Bowl

The 'Where We Are' Tour (2014)

The 'Where We Are' tour was One Direction's third headlining world tour and arguably their biggest, best and most successful so far. The band had reached full-blown superstar status, playing to sell-out crowds everywhere.

Where they played:

25	April	2014	Bogota, **Colombia** – Estadio El Campin
27	April	2014	Lima, **Peru** – Estadio Nacional
30	April	2014	Santiago, **Chile** – Estadio Nacional
1	May	2014	Santiago – Estadio Nacional
3	May	2014	Buenos Aires, **Argentina** – Estadio Velez Sarsfield
4	May	2014	Buenos Aires – Estadio Velez Sarsfield
6	May	2014	Montevideo, **Uruguay** – Estadio Centenario
8	May	2014	Rio de Janeiro, **Brazil** – Parque dos Atletas
10	May	2014	Sao Paulo – Estadio do Morumbi
11	May	2014	Sao Paulo – Estadio do Morumbi
23	May	2014	Dublin, **Ireland** – Croke Park
24	May	2014	Glasgow, **Scotland** – Glasgow Green
24	May	2014	Dublin, **Ireland** – Croke Park
25	May	2014	Dublin – Croke Park
28	May	2014	Sunderland, **England** – Stadium of Light
30	May	2014	Manchester Etihad Stadium
31	May	2014	Manchester Etihad Stadium
1	June	2014	Manchester Etihad Stadium
3	June	2014	Edinburgh, **Scotland** – Murrayfield Stadium
6	June	2014	London, **England** – Wembley Stadium
7	June	2014	London – Wembley Stadium
8	June	2014	London – Wembley Stadium
13	June	2014	Stockholm, **Sweden** – Friends Arena
14	June	2014	Stockholm – Friends Arena
16	June	2014	Copenhagen, **Denmark** – Parken Stadium
17	June	2014	Copenhagen – Parken Stadium
20	June	2014	Paris, **France** – Stade de France
21	June	2014	Paris – Stade de France
24	June	2014	Amsterdam, **Netherlands** – Amsterdam Arena
25	June	2014	Amsterdam – Amsterdam Arena

Oakland - Oracle Centre

28	June	2014	Milan, **Italy** – Stadio San Siro
29	June	2014	Milan – Stadio San Siro
2	July	2014	Dusseldorf, **Germany** – Esprit Arena
4	July	2014	Berne, **Switzerland** – Stade de Suisse
6	July	2014	Turin, **Italy** – Stadio Olimpico
8	July	2014	Barcelona, **Spain** – Estadi Olimpic
10	July	2014	Madrid – Estadio Vicente Calderon
11	July	2014	Madrid – Estadio Vicente Calderon
13	July	2014	Porto, **Portugal** – Estadio do Dragao
1	August	2014	Toronto, **Canada** – Rogers Centre
2	August	2014	Toronto – Rogers Centre
4	August	2014	East Rutherford, **USA** – MetLife Stadium
5	August	2014	East Rutherford – MetLife Stadium
7	August	2014	Foxboro – Gillette Stadium
8	August	2014	Foxboro – Gillette Stadium
9	August	2014	Foxboro – Gillette Stadium
11	August	2014	Washington D.C. – Nationals Park
13	August	2014	Philadelphia – Lincoln Financial Field
14	August	2014	Philadelphia – Lincoln Financial Field
16	August	2014	Detroit – Ford Field
17	August	2014	Detroit – Ford Field
19	August	2014	Nashville – LP Field
22	August	2014	Houston – Reliant Stadium
24	August	2014	Arlington – AT&T Stadium
27	August	2014	St. Louis – Edward Jones Dome
29	August	2014	Chicago – Soldier Field
30	August	2014	Chicago – Soldier Field
11 September	2014	Pasadena – Rose Bowl
12 September	2014	Pasadena – Rose Bowl

13 September	2014	Pasadena – Rose Bowl
16 September	2014	Glendale – Phoenix Stadium
19 September	2014	El Paso – Sun Bowl Stadium
21 September	2014	San Antonio – Alamodome
23 September	2014	Tulsa – BOK Center
25 September	2014	New Orleans – Mercedes-Benz Superdome
27 September	2014	Charlotte – PNC Music Pavilion
28 September	2014	Charlotte – PNC Music Pavilion
1	October	2014	Atlanta – Georgia Dome
3	October	2014	Tampa – Raymond James Stadium
5	October	2014	Miami – Sun Life Stadium

The 'On the Road Again' Tour (2015)

The 'On The Road Again' tour will be One Direction's fourth headlining stadium tour.

Where they are playing:

7	February	2015	Sydney, **Australia** – Allianz Stadium
8	February	2015	Sydney – Allianz Stadium
11	February	2015	Brisbane – Suncorp Stadium
14	February	2015	Melbourne – Etihad Stadium
15	February	2015	Melbourne – Etihad Stadium
17	February	2015	Adelaide – AAMI Stadium
20	February	2015	Perth – Patersons Stadium
24	February	2015	Osaka, **Japan** – Osaka Dome
25	February	2015	Osaka – Osaka Dome
27	February	2015	Tokyo – Saitama Super Arena
28	February	2015	Tokyo – Saitama Super Arena
1	March	2015	Tokyo – Saitama Super Arena
11	March	2015	Kallang, **Singapore** – Singapore National Stadium
14	March	2015	Bangkok, **Thailand** – Rajamangala Stadium
18	March	2015	**Hong Kong** – AsiaWorld Arena
21	March	2015	Manila, **Philippines** – Mall of Asia Concert Grounds
22	March	2015	Manila – Mall of Asia Concert Grounds
25	March	2015	Jakarta, **Indonesia** – Gelora Bung Karno Stadium
28	March	2015	Johannesburg, **South Africa** – FNB Stadium
29	March	2015	Johannesburg – FNB Stadium
1	April	2015	Cape Town – Cape Town Stadium
4	April	2015	Dubai, **United Arab Emirates** – Sevens Stadium

unich - Olympiahalle

The Support Acts

No One Direction concert would be complete without a fantastic support act to open the show and help to build excitement for what lies ahead. Here's the low-down on some of the amazing supporting artists from the tours so far...

Olly Murs – Olly Murs was the runner up in the sixth series of hit TV show *The X Factor* in 2009. Since then he has toured with One Direction and presented various TV shows including *The Xtra Factor* alongside Caroline Flack.

Boyce Avenue – Boyce Avenue are Alejandro Luis Manzano, Daniel Enrique Manzano and Fabian Rafael Manzano. These three brothers shot to fame on

YouTube and now release a mixture of popular cover tracks as well as their own independent music.

Matt Lonsdale – Matt Lonsdale is a singer/songwriter from the UK. He has become increasingly well known, especially across the social media network circuit, thanks to his hit cover videos of popular songs on YouTube.

Camryn – Camryn Magness is an American actress and pop singer from Denver, Colorado. She shot to fame on YouTube and has since toured with Cody Simpson and Grayson Chance as well as One Direction.

Manika – Manika is an Asian-Spanish American singer-songwriter and author. She was discovered by Michael Jackson's manager Frank DiLeo and has toured with One Direction and performed at the Hollywood Style Awards

Justice Crew – Justice Crew is an Australian hip-hop dance and pop music group. Bandmates Lukas 'Wildrok' Bellesini, Paul Eric Merciadez, John Len Ruela Pearce, Samson Cosray Smith and Solo

Tohi, formed the group in 2009 and went on to be crowned winners of the fourth season of *Australia's Got Talent*.

Johnny Ruffo – Johnny Ruffo is an Australian singer-songwriter, TV presenter, dancer and actor and a finalist on the third series of *The X Factor Australia* in 2011. In 2012 he went on to win the twelfth season of *Dancing with the Stars Australia*. Johnny Ruffo currently stars in the Australian soap opera *Home and Away* as Chris Harrington, making him a very busy, multi-talented guy.

Annah Mac – Annah Mac is a New Zealand singer-songwriter, producer and musician. Her most successful single to date is *Girl In Stilettos* which was certified Double Platinum in New Zealand.

5 Seconds of Summer – 5 Seconds of Summer opened the United Kingdom, North America, Australia and New Zealand tours for One Direction and have been busy building a hugely successful career for themselves ever since! Formed in Sydney in 2011, 5 Seconds of Summer consists of Luke

Hemmings (lead vocals, guitar), Michael Clifford (guitar, vocals), Calum Hood (bass guitar, vocals) and Ashton Irwin (drums, vocals). They initially rose to fame by uploading a series of popular cover tracks to their YouTube channel, gaining them a loyal fan-base.

Five Memorable Moments Tour

During the 'Take Me Home' tour Liam Payne had a very memorable moment when a fan managed to steal a pair of his Calvin Klein boxers after climbing up to his hotel room balcony!

While live on stage, Harry Styles got hit by a shoe. The whole incident was captured on camera by some of the fans in the audience and needless to say it didn't look as though it was one of Harry's favourite moments ever. Poor Harry!

The boys had a laugh with the 5 Seconds of Summer lads. They looked like they had a great time touring and performing on stage together and it seemed as though a real 'bromance' had been born.

Slips and trips – none of the guys have been seriously hurt, thank goodness, but there have been some pretty memorable stumbles on stage, most notably when water is involved! The boys are such pros though: they just get up and carry on.

Niall told a joke about a penguin on stage and it didn't quite get the side-splitting, rip-roaring reaction he'd hoped for. He was later mocked by his One Direction pals who told him he definitely needed to work on his delivery!

Albums

- *Up All Night* reached No.**2** in the UK Charts, sold **1,000,412** copies in the UK and **5,000,000** worldwide.

- *Take Me Home* reached No.**1** in the UK Charts, sold **906,000** copies in the UK and **5,000,000** worldwide.

- *Midnight Memories* reached No.**1** in the UK Charts, sold **726,000** copies in the UK and **4,000,000** worldwide.

Video Albums

- *One Direction - Up All Night, The Live Tour* reached No.**6** in the UK, sold **61,000** copies in the UK and **1,000,000** worldwide.

Singles

- *What Makes You Beautiful* - UK No.**1**
- *Gotta Be You* - UK No.**3**
- *One Thing* - UK No.**9**
- *More Than This* - UK No.**86**
- *Live While We're Young* - UK No.**3**
- *Little Things* - UK No.**1**
- *Kiss You* - UK No.**9**
- *One Way Or Another (Teenage Kicks)* - UK No.**1**
- *Best Song Ever* - UK No.**2**
- *Story Of My Life* - UK No.**2**
- *Midnight Memories* - UK No.**39**
- *You & I* - UK No.**19**
- *Heroes* - Featured Artist - UK No.**1**
- *Wishing On A Star* - Featured Artist - UK No.**1**

ALL ALBUM/SINGLE STATS CORRECT AS AT JULY 2014.

- One Direction have won **three** BRIT awards so far. They have also been nominated a further **three** times.

- Their debut single, *What Makes You Beautiful,* sold over **153,000** copies in the first **seven** days after release.

- One Direction have over **20 million** followers – and counting – on Twitter!

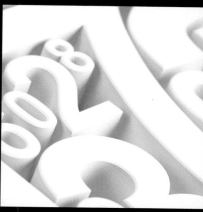

- One Direction have over **33 million** likes – and counting – on their official Facebook page!

- Their *Take Me Home* album reached Number **One** in **37** countries.

- *Midnight Memories* sold **237,000** copies in its first **seven** days on sale.

- Their debut album, *Up All Night*, reached Number **One** in **17** countries.

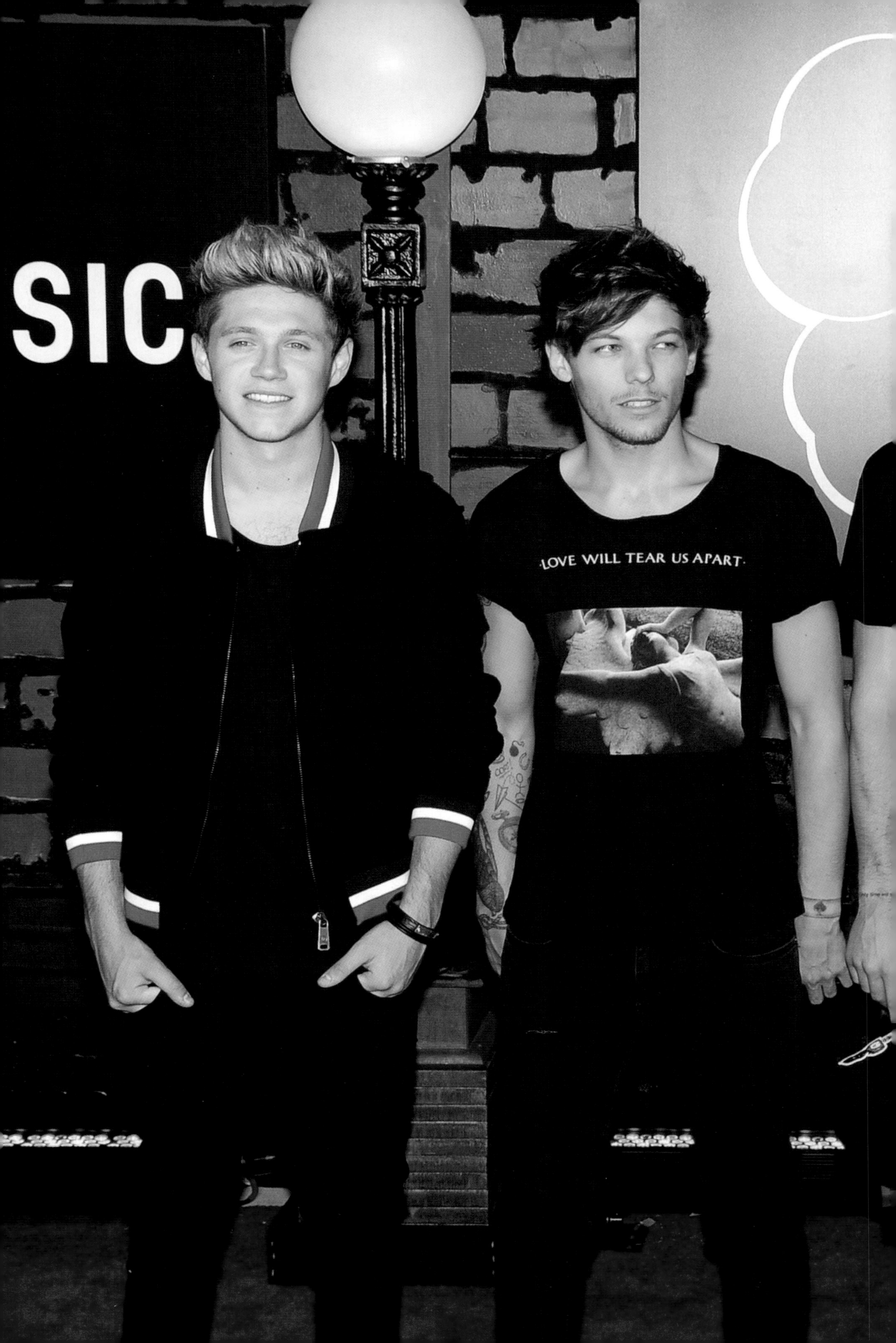
SIC
·LOVE WILL TEAR US APART·

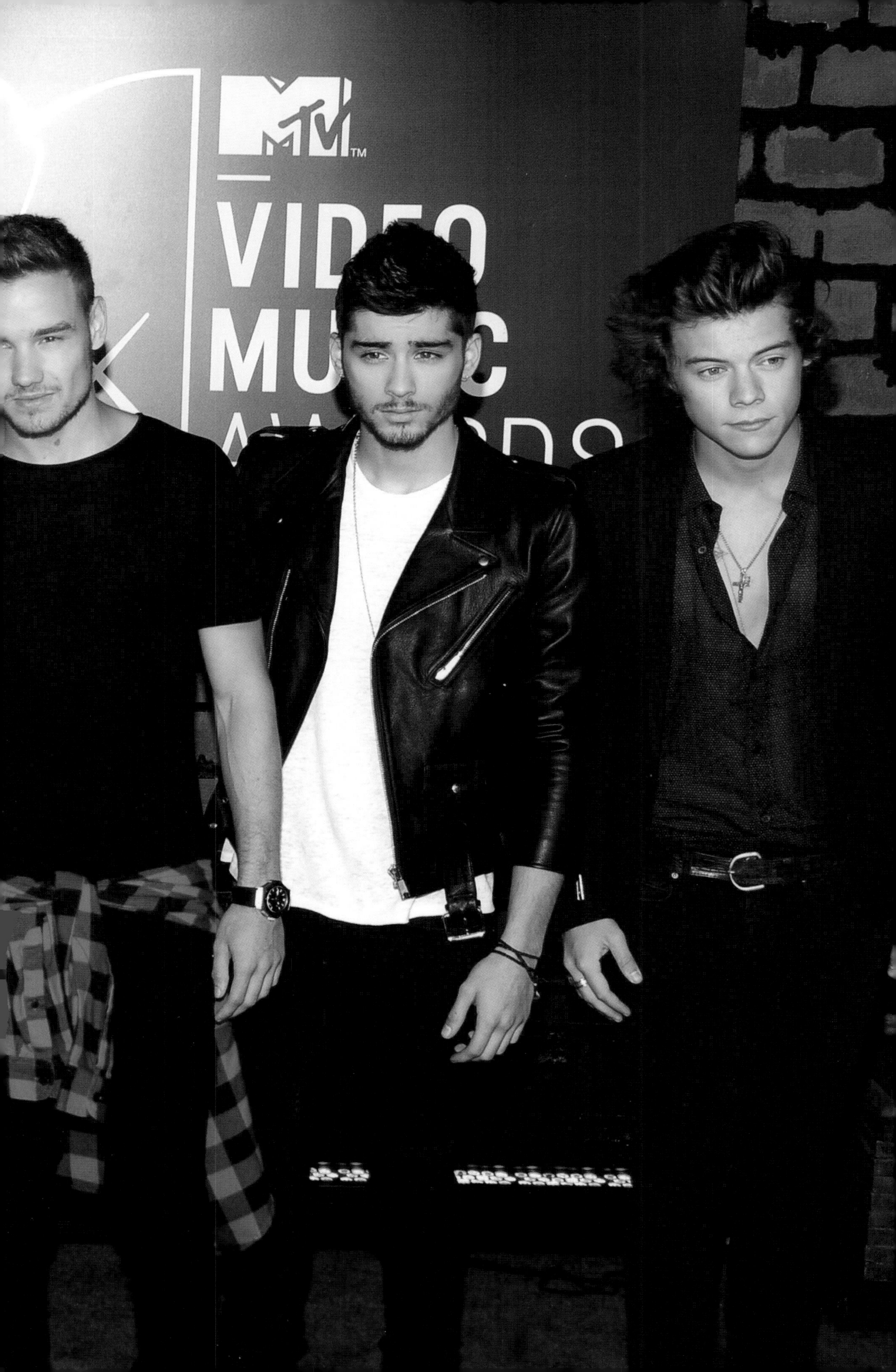
MTV
VIDEO

The **Big** One Direction Quiz

1. Which One Direction band member's nickname is 'Daddy Directioner'?

2. What was the name of One Direction's SECOND tour?

3. Who made a cameo appearance in the *One Way or Another (Teenage Kicks)* video as part of the comic relief tradition?

4. In the brilliantly inventive video for *You and I* what colour tops do the boys all wear?

5. Which single won the boys their first Brit Award?

6. Finish the official One Direction Harper Collins book title *One Direction: Forever* _____

7. Lifesize waxworks of the One Direction boys are displayed at popular tourist attraction _____ _____.

8. Who was once quoted in *Billboard* magazine getting all mushy by saying: "I have my four best mates on the road with me to keep me from getting lonely. Wouldn't give it up for anything."

9. When is Harry's birthday?

10. Liam and Harry stopped by which famous TV show in order to film themselves singing the ABC song with classic character 'Bert'?

11. Liam has recently become besties with which 'Happy' singer?

12. Which instrument does Niall play best?

13. Harry has recently been receiving lessons to play which instrument?

14. When is Zayn's birthday?

15. What is the name of Simon Cowell's record label?

16. Finish the hit single title: *Live* ____ _____ ____.

17. What was One Direction's SECOND studio album called?

18. As part of Comic Relief, One Direction travelled to ____ to visit a children's hospital and school there.

19. What was the release date of the *Midnight Memories* album?

20. When is Louis' birthday?

ANSWERS ON PAGE 61

Sporty Lads!

One Direction are one of the most sporty, physically fit bands you'll ever meet. All of the boys have their own favourite sports to play and watch. Here are a few of their top sporting-related moments…

Louis and Football

Louis Tomlinson is a keen football player and supporter. He even launched a campaign in 2014 with Crowdfunder to support Doncaster Rovers Football Club - a team very close to his heart.

Louis, who plays for the Doncaster Rovers Reserves, recently set up the trust with businessman and ex-Doncaster Rovers Chairman, John Ryan. Explaining why they decided to launch a crowdfunding campaign Louis commented on www.crowdfunder.co.uk:
"For me, this is all about the football, the community and restoring the excitement and desire to making Doncaster Rovers the most exciting club to play for in Yorkshire. I want to see the Doncaster Rovers supporters get the club the success it deserves. I grew up in Doncaster and have felt the love for football run through the town, it's for that reason that I have a real personal passion to make Doncaster Rovers a success story. This is a big step which I believe will open up opportunities to provide a very, very exciting future for the club and its supporters."

Harry and Tennis

In some '1D Day' (YouTube.com) footage Harry can be seen getting very into a game of tennis with Pat Raftner – former World No. 1 tennis player. In other sports news, Harry is also a big Manchester United football supporter.

Liam and Surfing

Liam loves to surf. In the '1D Day' (YouTube.com) sports footage he says, "Sometimes you do just want your own personal time and personal space." He goes on to say that sometimes, being able to enjoy the sunshine and the sea is a great escape. He's pretty good on a surfboard and isn't afraid to tackle a few big waves!

Niall and Football or Rugby

Niall is really into football and rugby. One of his favourite moments was when he got to play with international rugby player Quade Cooper and the team outside the tour bus in 2013.

Zayn and Manchester United

Despite being from Bradford, Zayn is a huge Manchester United supporter just like his fellow band-mates Harry and Louis. Zayn often enjoys a kick-about with the rest of the One Direction lads and never passes up a chance to catch his favourite team on the big screen.

The boys all also enjoy relaxing and taking some time out on tour for a good game of volleyball on a local beach, some skateboarding or a round of golf.

Favourite Food and Drinks

One Direction have to keep themselves fit and healthy on tour so it is important that they get a good variety of food that is good for them as well as the occasional treat. They might be lucky enough to have their own personal chef who cooks for them on tour, but even One Direction have to have a 'cheat day' when they can scoff whatever food they fancy.

Harry

Harry is usually working on his fitness and building up those muscles! His favourite foods include lots of meat for protein but he'll usually still find time for a trip to Nandos or a local pizza place, we're sure!

Liam

Liam seems to be a bit more health conscious. He enjoys steak, bacon and lots of vegetables and salad to keep his immune system healthy and strong.

Louis

Louis is easily pleased and will happily settle for a bowl of Kellogg's Special K if nothing else is available. Failing that he'll eat whatever the rest of the band happens to be having. He's definitely not a demanding foodie then!

Niall

Niall is a comfort food kind of guy. He enjoys pie and mash, sausage and mash, creamy chicken pasta and chicken kievs. Not all at once we hope!

Zayn

Zayn also likes to keep it simple and quick. He especially enjoys pasta Bolognese or spicy chicken.

Drinks

The One Direction lads usually keep things a no-booze zone. They prefer to drink things like tea, water, juices, smoothies and the occasional soda. After all, they do have to keep themselves perfectly hydrated if they're going to be running around on stage every night!

Discography

One Direction's discography seems to be growing at a seriously fast pace. Their hit singles, albums and videos earn them much critical acclaim and this fab fivesome are always writing and recording potential new hits to keep fans entertained.

Albums

Up All Night (2011)
Take Me Home (2012)
Midnight Memories (2013)

Singles

What Makes You Beautiful
Up All Night
Gotta Be You
One Thing
More Than This
Live While We're Young
Take Me Home
Little Things
Kiss You
One Way or Another (Teenage Kicks)
Best Song Ever
Midnight Memories
Story of My Life
You & I

As featured artists:
Heroes
Wishing on a Star

Videos

Heroes - As part of *The X Factor* Finalists 2010
What Makes You Beautiful
Gotta Be You
Wishing on a Star - *The X Factor* Finalists 2011 featuring JLS and One Direction
One Thing
More Than This
Live While We're Young
Little Things
Kiss You
One Way or Another (Teenage Kicks)
Best Song Ever
Story of My Life
Midnight Memories
You & I

Showbiz Buddies

When you've become high flying superstars like One Direction have, it's easy to become friends with fellow A-list stars and celebrities. Here are some of the famous faces that the One Direction lads have been spotted hanging out with.

Pharrell Williams

Lately it seems that Pharrell Williams and Liam Payne have become firm celeb pals. Liam reportedly stopped by Pharrell's studio a few times and there are even rumours that these guys may be keen to collaborate on musical projects together in the future.

Olly Murs

Olly has toured with the boys on various occasions and these cheeky chaps all seem to have fun, laid back personalities that just gel perfectly. We bet that tour bus pranks aplenty happened when these guys got together!

Nick Grimshaw

Radio 1 DJ Nick 'Grimmy' Grimshaw is firm friends with the boys and has a particularly great friendship with Harry Styles. The two are often spotted out and about together and always look to be on good terms.

Little Mix

Zayn Malik and Perrie Edwards' relationship has probably meant that One Direction and Little Mix have also become quite a close knit duo of bands. What do you think.... could a musical collaboration ever happen between these two pop groups?

Cher Lloyd

Cher is a huge fan of One Direction as well as being their showbiz pal! She told Yahoo! Celebrity: "We're both always all over the place trying to work hard and trying to get somewhere, so I've seen a lot of them on the Internet and on TV, and it's great they're doing so well. It kind of sets it up for me, too. You know, if someone else can do it from a TV show, then I can do it, too. It's hard for anyone to break into this music industry, and I think having a collective bunch of people makes it slightly easier - and the guys, too. Girls love guys [laughs] … I'm very much a One Direction fan. I think they're the best boys out there right now."

Ed Sheeran

One Direction are all self-confessed fans of Ed Sheeran's music and Ed has even penned some tracks for the boys. Harry and Ed also have an ex-girlfriend in common - they've both dated Taylor Swift.

Simon Cowell

Simon Cowell seems to be really good mates with the One Direction lads. They seem to have a good working relationship as well as having developed a solid friendship over the years. His music know-how has been invaluable to the boys and Simon only ever has good things to say about them!

Fashion and Style Focus

One Direction have come a long way since their early days on *The X Factor*. This has been reflected in their own individual personalities, their confidence as a band and also in their sense of fashion and style throughout their career.

One Direction have grown up in the public eye. Throughout the last few years of their whirlwind musical career we've seen their style change from that of a typical teenage boy-band to that of a group of stylish, confident young men.

The boys are not afraid to get their glad-rags on and get dressed up these days. They are regularly spotted rocking seriously suave suit and jacket combos. Sometimes we'll see them fully dressed up with ties and stylish loafers. On other occasions we'll see them completely dress-down their smart but wearable look simply by leaving their collars unbuttoned a little and opting for some comfy, casual trainers instead.

During the warmer months One Direction seem to be big fans of casual t-shirts, shorts and surf-style beachwear. Liam in such as 'Toms' which are comfortable to wear and seem perfectly suited for a day spent running around from location to location. All of the boys definitely know exactly what outfit, hairstyle and look suits them best and they've successfully avoided any

particular is really into his lumberjack shirts though and is a huge fan of brands like Superdry and G-Star Raw.

All of the boys are regularly spotted wearing their hi-top Converse trainers but are equally in to eco-friendly footwear brands

major fashion faux-pas so far. With Liam regularly being compared to style god David Beckham and Harry and the rest of the boys looking more handsome by the day, they are almost certainly set to be one of those bands that mature tastefully with age!

Charity Work

One Direction are well known for their involvement with charities and their desire to give back to those less fortunate than themselves. The band have strong ties with charities such as Comic Relief and have even visited orphanages and schools in poverty-stricken locations around the world, in a bid to highlight their desperate need for our help. One Direction were even named among 2013's Most Charitable Stars alongside Taylor Swift by social change organization DoSomething.org.

Here are some of One Direction's other philanthropic involvements and ways in which they try to help charities and communities who may be struggling.

BBC Children in Need

One Direction performed on the 'BBC Children in Need' 2011 broadcast, helping raise over £26 million. In 2012 they further extended their involvement with the

charity as they opened the telecast with a performance of their single 'Live While We're Young'. The group said it was "incredible" to be involved in the charity event as it was something that they had "always watched as children".

Ambassadors for the Children's Charity Rays of Sunshine

Rays of Sunshine are a charity that helps grant the wishes of seriously ill children. One Direction are ambassadors for Rays of Sunshine and are only too happy to meet the children and spend time with them to make a life-long wish come true for some of these children. Rays of Sunshine was first founded

in 2003 in order to help children who are living with serious or life-limiting illnesses between the ages of 3-18, in the UK.

Cancer Charity Trekstock

Harry Styles and Liam Payne turned two fans' dreams into reality when they won a competition organised by Trekstock to have lunch with Harry and Liam.

Harry said: "We're really excited to be working with the guys at Trestock on something so unique… We're proud to be ambassadors." (trestock.com)

Trekstock aims to help beat cancer through funding research of the highest standard and ensuring all young people have the right and relevant information to make better informed lifestyle choices.

Kids in a New Groove 'Kicks for Kids'

One Direction helped out with this worthy cause in 2013 by donating their shoes for charity; the 'Kicks for Kids' contest featured all five band members' autographed pairs of shoes in a virtual online race to reach the highest bid. The highest bidder for each pair won that band member's shoe and the winner of the pair with the highest total bid also won a CD signed by the entire band. Kids in a New Groove provides Texas youth in foster care with a committed one-on-one mentoring relationship through weekly private music instruction.

Stand Up To Cancer

Channel 4 and Cancer Research UK joined forces

to launch Stand Up To Cancer in the UK. The generous One Direction lads pledged £200,000 of ticket profits made during their 'Where We Are' 2014 tour to Stand Up To Cancer. The non-profit organisation brings together the brightest stars in the world of entertainment to help beat cancer sooner.

Alzheimer's Society

One Direction showed their support for this charity by donating a signed t-shirt that was auctioned on eBay. Louis started supporting the charity after his girlfriend Eleanor Calder's grandfather was diagnosed with dementia. Alzheimer's Society is the leading UK care and research charity for people with this disease and other dementias, their families and carers.

The Covers

As well as writing and singing their own selection of fantastic songs, One Direction have also been known to put their stamp on some classic tracks. Take a look at some of the best, below, and see if you can find your favourite.

One Way or Another (Teenage Kicks)

In 2013, One Direction recorded a cover of *One Way or Another (Teenage Kicks)* that was released as the official Comic Relief record. What a great way to resurrect a classic song and help raise money for charity in the process.

About the original:

The track was originally recorded by Blondie - an American rock band founded by singer Debbie Harry and guitarist Chris Stein. The band was a pioneer in the early American new wave and punk scenes of the mid-1970s.

Teenage Dirtbag

One Direction sang a cover of the song during their Take Me Home tour in 2013. It reached number two in the UK and Germany.

About the original:

The original is by Wheatus - an American rock group from Northport, New York, who formed in 1995. The song was also used in the movie *Loser* and the HBO series *Generation Kill*.

Hey There Delilah

Louis Tomlinson covered this track for his audition in season seven of *The X Factor* in 2010 and it sounded amazing.

About the original:

The original is by Plain White T's - an American pop punk band from Villa Park, Illinois. They were formed in 1997 by high school friends Tom Higgenson, Dave Tirio, Ken Fletcher and Steve Mast. The No. 1 hit song *Hey There Delilah* achieved platinum status in 2007 and earned two Grammy nominations.

All You Need Is Love

In 2010, One Direction performed *All You Need Is Love* on the live show in week seven of the seventh series of *The X Factor*.

About the original:

All You Need Is Love was written by John Lennon and credited to Lennon-McCartney. It was first performed by The Beatles on *Our World*, the first live global television link.

Pop-up Stores

The following cities have played host to One Direction World Stores:

AFRICA
Johannesburg
AUSTRALIA
Brisbane
Melbourne
Perth
Adelaide
Sydney
CANADA
Calgary
Toronto
Vancouver
Edmonton
ENGLAND
Leeds
ITALY
Milan
JAPAN
Sendai
Kumamoto
Shizuoka
NORWAY
Oslo
PORTUGAL
Lisbon
SCOTLAND
Glasgow
SPAIN
Madrid
Barcelona
SWEDEN
Stockholm
USA
Chicago
New York City
Minneapolis
Boston
Phoenix

One Direction's huge popularity worldwide makes them seriously marketable. Fans everywhere are desperate to get their hands on some official One Direction merchandise and goodies and One Direction World pop-up stores are the perfect way to do this.

As the name suggests, 'pop-up' stores are set up for a limited time only, usually on or around the Christmas and festive months and these allow fans to get a quick One Direction fix for a limited time frame. The stores sell everything from cardboard cut-outs of the band to music, t-shirts and memorabilia that is fit for any One Direction fanatic.

Look out for a pop-up store opening near you...!

SPOT THE DIFFERENCE

Take a look at the two pictures of One Direction below. Notice anything different or out of the ordinary between the two? Circle the differences and check your answers at the back of the book to see how well your One Direction observational skills are shaping up!

CROSSWORD

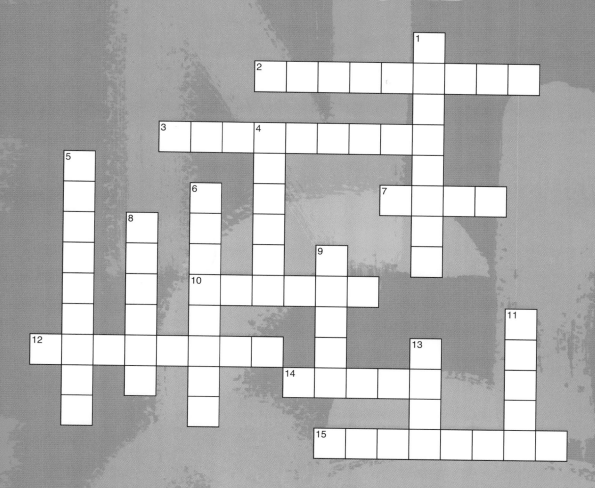

ACROSS

2 Niall's home town in Ireland. (9)

3 The name of One Direction's fragrance. (3,6)

7 One Direction member who broke his toe by dropping his computer on it. (4)

10 Comic _____ - charity One Direction sang *One Way Or Another (Teenage Kicks)* for. (6)

12 Zayn's home town. (8)

14 One Direction member who stole soap from Johnny Depp's bathroom. (5)

15 *Midnight* _____ - One Direction album. (8)

DOWN

1 The video for this song features a London bus and space hoppers. (3,5)

4 The name of the marketing man in *Best Song Ever* video. (6)

5 Artist who wrote *Little Things* for One Direction. (2,7)

6 Morgan _____, the director of One Direction's *This Is Us* movie. (8)

8 Zayn's middle name. (6)

9 Harry's sister's name. (5)

11 Michael _____. Niall's favourite singer. (5)

13 One Direction's music label. (4)

ANSWERS ON PAGE 61

Awards & Nominations

American Music Awards:
2012 Favourite Pop/Rock Album - Nominated (Up All Night)
2012 Favourite Group - Nominated
2012 New Artist Of The Year - Nominated
2013 Favourite Pop/Rock Album - **Winners**
2013 Favourite Group - **Winners**

Aria Music Awards:
2012 Best International Act - **Winners**
2013 Best International Act - **Winners**

Bambi Awards:
2012 Pop International - **Winners**

BBC Radio 1 Teen Awards:
2012 Best British Album (Up All Night) - **Winners**
2012 Best British Music Act - **Winners**
2012 Best British Single (One Thing) - **Winners**
2013 Best British Group - **Winners**
2013 Best British Single (Best Song Ever) - **Winners**

Bravo Otto:
2012 Super Band - Nominated
2013 Super Band - **Winners**
2013 Super Internet Star - Nominated

Billboard Music Awards:
2013 Billboard 200 Album (Take Me Home) - Nominated
2013 Billboard 200 Album (Up All Night) - Nominated
2013 Top Pop Album (Take Me Home) - Nominated
2013 Top Pop Album (Up All Night) - Nominated
2013 Artist Of The Year - Nominated
2013 Top Billboard 200 Artist - Nominated
2013 Top Social Artist - Nominated
2013 Top Duo/Group - **Winners**
2013 New Artist Of The Year - **Winners**
2013 Top Pop Artist - **Winners**

Billboard Touring Awards:
2013 Concert Marketing & Promo - Nominated
2013 Breakthrough - Winners

Brit Awards:
2012 Best Single (What Makes You Beautiful) - **Winners**
2013 British Group - Nominated
2013 Brits Global Success - **Winners**
2014 British Single (One Way Or Another (Teenage Kicks)) - Nominated
2014 British Group - Nominated
2014 British Video (Best Song Ever) - **Winners**
2014 Brits Global Success - **Winners**

MTV VIDEO MUSIC AWARDS 2012

MTV VIDEO MUSIC AWARDS 2012

Capricho Awards:

2011 International Development - Nominated
2012 Best Book *(Dare To Dream)* - **Winners**
2012 Best Cover Of Capricho - **Winners**
2012 Best Video *(Live While We're Young)* - **Winners**
2012 International Band - **Winners**
2012 International Male Hottie (Harry Styles) - Nominated
2012 International Hit *(What Makes You Beautiful)* - **Winners**
2013 Bapho Of The Year (Harry Styles & Taylor Swift) - Nominated
2013 Best Real Couple (Zayn Malik & Perrie Edwards) - **Winners**
2013 Best Twitter (Niall Horan) - Nominated
2013 International Band - **Winners**
2013 International Male Hottie (Liam Payne) - **Winners**
2013 Year's Fan Club (Directioners) - **Winners**

Do Something Awards:

2012 Music Artist - Nominated

The Fragrance Foundation (FiFi) Awards:

2014 Best New Commercial – Female Fragrance (Our Moment) - Nominated
2014 Best New Celebrity Fragrance (Our Moment) - Nominated
2014 Best New Female Fragrance (Our Moment) - Nominated
2014 Ultimate Launch (Our Moment) - **Winners**

Golden Trailer Awards:

2012 Best Trailer, No Movie *(Up All Night Live Tour)* - Nominated

Japan Golden Disc Awards:

2013 New Western Artist Of The Year - **Winners**
2014 Artist Of The Year - **Winners**
2014 Album Of The Year *(Take Me Home)* - **Winners**
2014 One Of The Best Three Albums In Western Music - **Winners**

JIM Awards:

2012 Best Newcomer (INTL) - **Winners**
2013 Best Group - **Winners**
2013 Best Pop - **Winners**
2013 Hottie Of The Year (Harry Styles) - Nominated
2014 Best International Band - **Winners**
2014 Best International Album - Nominated
2014 Best Dressed Male (Harry Styles) - **Winners**

Juno Awards:

2013 International Album *(Up All Night)* - Nominated
2014 International Album *(Take Me Home)* - Nominated

MTV:

2012 Artist Of The Year - **Winners**
2012 Best European Act (EMA) - Nominated
2012 Best New Act (EMA) - **Winners**
2012 Best UK & Ireland Act (EMA) - **Winners**
2012 Biggest Fans (EMA) - **Winners**
2012 Best New Artist (VMA) - **Winners**
2012 Best Pop Video (VMA – *What Makes You Beautiful)* - **Winners**
2012 Most Share-Worthy Video (VMA – *What Makes You Beautiful)* - **Winners**

BAMBI AWARDS 2012

MTV VIDEO MUSIC AWARDS 2013

2012 International Artist (Brazilian VMA) - **Winners**
2012 Best Fans (Italian VMA) - Nominated
2013 Artist Of The Year - **Winners**
2013 Best Look (EMA – Harry Styles) - **Winners**
2013 Best North European Act (EMA) - **Winners**
2013 Best Pop (EMA) - **Winners**
2013 Best UK & Ireland Act (EMA) - **Winners**

AMERICAN MUSIC AWARDS 2013

2013 Best Worldwide Act (EMA) - Nominated
2013 Biggest Fans (EMA) - Nominated
2013 Hottest Summer Superstar - **Winners**
2013 MTV's Star - **Winners**
2013 Best Song Of The Summer *(Best Song Ever)* - **Winners**

MTV VIDEO MUSIC AWARDS 2013

Look to the Future

One Direction's career has gone from strength to strength as the years have gone by.

The boys have visited every country they could ever hope to see, immersed themselves in different cultures and entertained fans from various backgrounds and all walks of life.

One Direction have gone from being just a band on our TV screens during *The X Factor*, to becoming a household name in their own right. Movies have been made about them, books have been published documenting their epic career and they even boast an army of loyal fans who support every new and exciting venture that the boys undertake.

With their *On The Road Again* tour set to keep them perfectly in the public eye throughout the whole of 2015, there's no chance of One Direction stopping or even slowing down any time soon as they continue their staggering ascent in to musical stardom.

BRIT AWARDS 2014

Answers

ANAGRAMS p19

1. BEST SONG EVER
2. LITTLE THINGS
3. STORY OF MY LIFE
4. LITTLE BLACK DRESS
5. GOTTA BE YOU
6. ANOTHER WORLD
7. SUMMER LOVE
8. IRRESISTIBLE
9. LAST FIRST KISS

WORDSEARCH p22

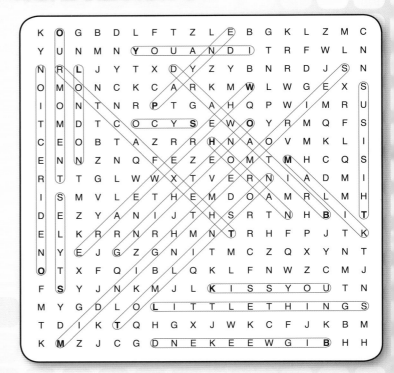

SPOT THE DIFFERENCE p23

THE BIG ONE DIRECTION QUIZ p34

1. LIAM
2. THE 'TAKE ME HOME' TOUR
3. DAVID CAMERON
4. GREY
5. WHAT MAKES YOU BEAUTIFUL
6. YOUNG
7. MADAME TUSSAUDS
8. NIALL
9. 1ST FEBRUARY
10. SESAME STREET
11. PHARRELL WILLIAMS
12. GUITAR
13. THE PIANO
14. 12TH JANUARY
15. SYCO
16. 'LIVE WHILE WE'RE YOUNG'
17. TAKE ME HOME
18. GHANA
19. 25TH NOVEMBER 2013
20. 24TH DECEMBER

CROSSWORD p55

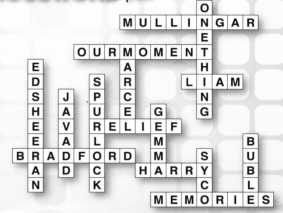

SPOT THE DIFFERENCE p54

Where are the boys?

We've hidden Harry, Louis, Zayn, Liam and Niall in the crowd – can you spot them all?